Cockroaches Up Close

Robin Birch

www.raintreepublishers.co.uk

Visit our website to find out more information about **Raintree** books.

To order:
☎ Phone 44 (0) 1865 888112
📄 Send a fax to 44 (0) 1865 314091
💻 Visit the Raintree Bookshop at **www.raintreepublishers.co.uk** to browse our catalogue and order online.

Published in 2004 by Heinemann Library
a division of Harcourt Education Australia,
18–22 Salmon Street, Port Melbourne Victoria 3207 Australia
(a division of Reed International Books Australia Pty Ltd,
ABN 70 001 002 357).
Visit the Heinemann Library website @
www.heinemannlibrary.com.au

First published in Great Britain by Raintree,
Halley Court, Jordan Hill, Oxford OX2 8EJ,
part of Harcourt Education.
Raintree is a registered trademark of Harcourt Education Ltd.

℞ A Reed Elsevier company

© Reed International Books Australia Pty Ltd 2004

08 07 06 05 04
10 9 8 7 6 5 4 3 2 1

Editorial: Carmel Heron, Anne McKenna
Design: Stella Vassiliou, Marta White
Photo research: Jes Senbergs, Wendy Duncan
Illustration: Rob Mancini
Production: Tracey Jarrett

Typeset in Officina Sans 19/23 pt
Pre-press by Digital Imaging Group (DIG)
Printed in China by WKT Company Ltd.

The paper used to print this book comes from sustainable resources.

National Library of Australia Cataloguing-in-Publication data:

Birch, Robin.
    Cockroaches up close.

    Includes index.
    For primary students.
    ISBN 1 74070 190 9.

    1. Cockroaches - Juvenile literature. I. Title.
    (Series : Birch, Robin. Minibeasts up close).

595.728

Acknowledgements
The publisher would like to thank the following for permission to
reproduce photographs: AAP: p. **29**; Auscape/Kathie Atkinson:
pp. **12, 20, 25**; Australian Museum: p. **19**; Bruce Coleman
Inc./Adrian Davis: p. **28**; Corbis/APL/Jim Zuckerman: p. **13**,
Getty Images/Stone: p. **17**; Natural Visions/Heather Angel:
p. **10**; Lochman Transparencies/© Jiri Lochman: pp. **5, 14, 15,
21, 24, 26, 27**, /David Knowles: p. **7**; National Geographic:
p. **11**; © Paul Zborowski: p. **6**; © Queensland Museum/Jeff Wright:
p. **16**; Science Photo Library/Gusto: p. **4**, /David Scharf: p. **8**.

Cover photograph of an American cockroach reproduced
with permission of Queensland Museum/Jeff Wright.

Every attempt has been made to trace and acknowledge
copyright. Where an attempt has been unsuccessful, the
publisher would be pleased to hear from the copyright owner
so any omission or error can be rectified.

Contents

Any words appearing in bold, **like this**, are explained in the Glossary.

Amazing cockroaches!

Have you seen a cockroach? Was that cockroach running so fast you could not see what it was?

Cockroaches are amazing when you get to know them, close up. They will eat almost anything! They are sometimes pests in houses, because they get into food and leave a smelly mess behind them.

Some cockroaches enter houses to look for food.

What are cockroaches?

Cockroaches are insects. An insect has six legs. It also has a hard skin on the outside of its body called an **exoskeleton**, instead of bones inside its body.

Smelly spray

Stinking cockroaches hide under piles of wood on the ground. If they are disturbed, they spray a burning, smelly mist to protect themselves against **predators**.

There are nearly 4000 kinds, or **species**, of cockroaches in the world. The smallest is about as long as a large sesame seed (2.5 millimetres). The largest is about as long as a computer mouse (10 centimetres).

Cockroaches are beetle-like insects.

5

Where do cockroaches live?

Most **species** of cockroaches live in warm, moist places.

Cockroaches often live in forests, where they can find food easily. Some cockroaches live in caves, holes in rocks and in hollow trees. They find food that has fallen into their home. Some live in rotting wood, and eat it. Some cockroaches live some of the time in water. They can swim and dive.

Cockroaches are flat insects, which makes it easy for them to squeeze through narrow gaps.

How do they live?

Most cockroaches are **nocturnal** and hide during the day. They find a small space to rest in, such as under stones, logs or bark. They search for food and water at night. Most cockroaches stay near the ground.

Some cockroaches live in dry deserts. At night they stick their tongues out to collect moisture from the air.

Some kinds of cockroaches run in the treetops, in the daytime.

Tiny cockroaches

Attaphila (at-a-<u>fill</u>-a) *fungicola* (fung-gee-<u>cole</u>-a) cockroaches are about as long as a large sesame seed (2.5 millimetres). They live underground in ant nests. They ride on the backs of ants in the nest and on ants flying through the forest.

Cockroach body parts

Most cockroaches have wide, flat bodies. A cockroach body has three parts. These are the head, the **thorax** and the **abdomen** (<u>ab</u>-da-men).

The head

The head has eyes, mouthparts and feelers called **antennae** (an-<u>ten</u>-ay) on it. The head bends downwards.

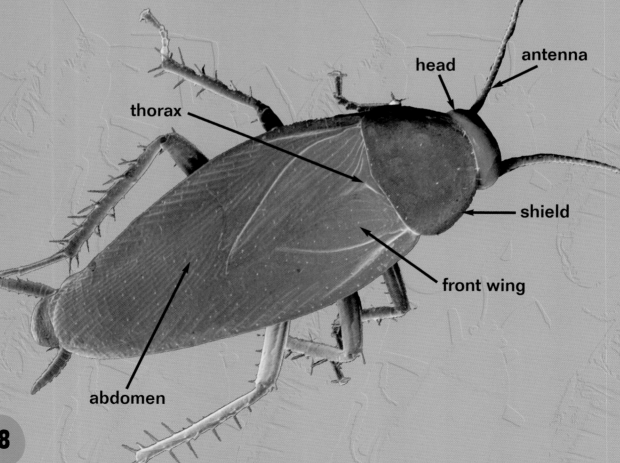

head

antenna

thorax

shield

front wing

abdomen

The thorax

The thorax has six legs on it. Most cockroaches have four wings attached to the thorax as well. The cockroach has a **shield** on the back of its thorax.

The abdomen

A cockroach's abdomen is usually covered by its wings, so we cannot see it.

The exoskeleton

The **exoskeleton** covers the whole of a cockroach's body, even its eyes. It is about as thick as a person's hair. The exoskeleton makes the cockroach's shape. It protects the cockroach from being hurt, and stops it from drying out by trapping water inside its body. There are hairs and **spines** on the exoskeleton.

Mouthparts and eating

Cockroaches eat almost any kind of food. They eat leaves and fruit on trees. In forests, they clean up the forest floor by eating dead and rotting plants and animals. They are good hunters, and catch insects such as termites, flies, wasps and mosquitoes.

In houses, they like sweet things, such as bread and biscuits. Cockroaches may also eat old books and wallpaper.

Cockroaches eat almost anything, including books!

Jaws

Cockroaches have two large, strong **jaws**, one on each side of the mouth. The jaws open and close sideways, and they have strong teeth on the ends.

Cockroaches have two smaller jaws, inside the others. They clean their **antennae** (feelers) and legs with these jaws.

Palps

Cockroaches have four small **palps**, like fingers, under their mouths, two on each side. Cockroaches feel and taste their food with the palps before they eat it.

Cockroaches use their palps to feel and taste food.

11

Eyes and seeing

A cockroach has two large eyes. Each eye is made of 2000 very small eyes. This kind of eye is called a **compound** eye. The small eyes are all packed closely together. Each small eye faces in a slightly different direction, and sees something a little bit different from the other small eyes.

All cockroaches have two large eyes, one on each side of the head.

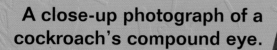

A close-up photograph of a cockroach's compound eye.

Cockroaches do not see very well. They know what is happening around them by smelling, feeling and hearing.

Extra eyes

Many cockroaches also have two tiny eyes, one above each compound eye. These eyes probably only see light and dark. Scientists think these eyes may help a cockroach when it is flying.

Antennae and sensing

A cockroach has two long feelers called **antennae** on its head to **sense** with. The antennae are as long as the cockroach's body.

Sensing with antennae

A cockroach touches and smells things with its antennae. The antennae sense the **temperature** around the cockroach. This means it can stay away from places that are too hot or too cold. A cockroach senses movement nearby with its antennae, so it can run away if it needs to.

A cockroach can move its antennae right around itself.

Cleaning antennae

Cockroaches pull their antennae through their mouth so they are cleaned by hairs on the inside jaws.

More senses

Cockroaches have ears in their knees, which can hear very soft sounds. They also have **spines** and hairs on their legs that can feel movements in the air and in the ground.

Cockroaches can taste and smell food with their feet.

15

Legs for moving

Cockroaches have six legs joined to the **thorax**. Each leg has three main parts, and a long foot. The legs are hairy and covered with **spines**.

How cockroaches move

When a cockroach runs and walks, it moves three legs at a time. The front and back legs on one side step forward at the same time as the middle leg on the other side.

Cockroaches are fast runners. For their size, they can run ten times faster than a person!

Cockroach feet

Each foot has two large claws on the end. Cockroaches also have sticky pads on their feet and front legs. These help them run fast on smooth, slippery surfaces.

Sensing with feet

Cockroaches have hairs on their feet that feel **vibrations** in the air and in the ground. They run away very suddenly if they feel anything move near them.

Cockroaches pull themselves up with their claws, when they climb.

17

Wings and flying

Many cockroaches are strong fliers. They fly to look for food. Flying cockroaches have four wings. **Veins** in the wings keep the shape of the cockroach's wings. The veins are hard, hollow tubes.

Cockroaches fold their wings back over their bodies when they are not using them. The back wings are hidden underneath the front wings. The front wings protect the back wings.

Running fast

Brownbanded cockroaches run very fast by spreading their wings, and running on their back legs. The air on the wings pushes the end of the body down, making the back legs work better.

Flying

The front wings are thick and the same colour as the rest of the cockroach. The cockroach lifts them out of the way while it is flying, and flies with its back wings. These are very thin, and clear.

Flying cockroaches have two wings on each side of the **thorax**.

The thorax and abdomen

A cockroach's **thorax** has legs and wings joined onto it. There is a **shield** on the back of the thorax.

The **abdomen** has two cerci (<u>ser</u>-see), like small tail fingers, on the end. If the cerci sense movement, the cockroach's legs start running before it even knows that something is there.

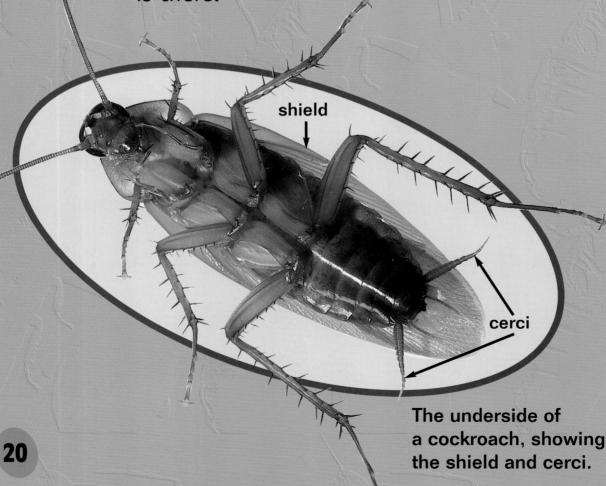

shield

cerci

The underside of a cockroach, showing the shield and cerci.

Many cockroaches have interesting colours and patterns on their shield.

Making sounds

Cockroaches sometimes make squeaking sounds by rubbing the hard edges of the front wings on the back end of the shield on the thorax.

Some cockroaches make a tapping noise by banging their abdomens on the ground.

Singing cockroaches

Male cinereous (sie-near-i-us) cockroaches make singing sounds to attract a female. Both the males and females make a squeaky sound if they are disturbed. They make the sounds with their wings and the shield on their thorax.

21

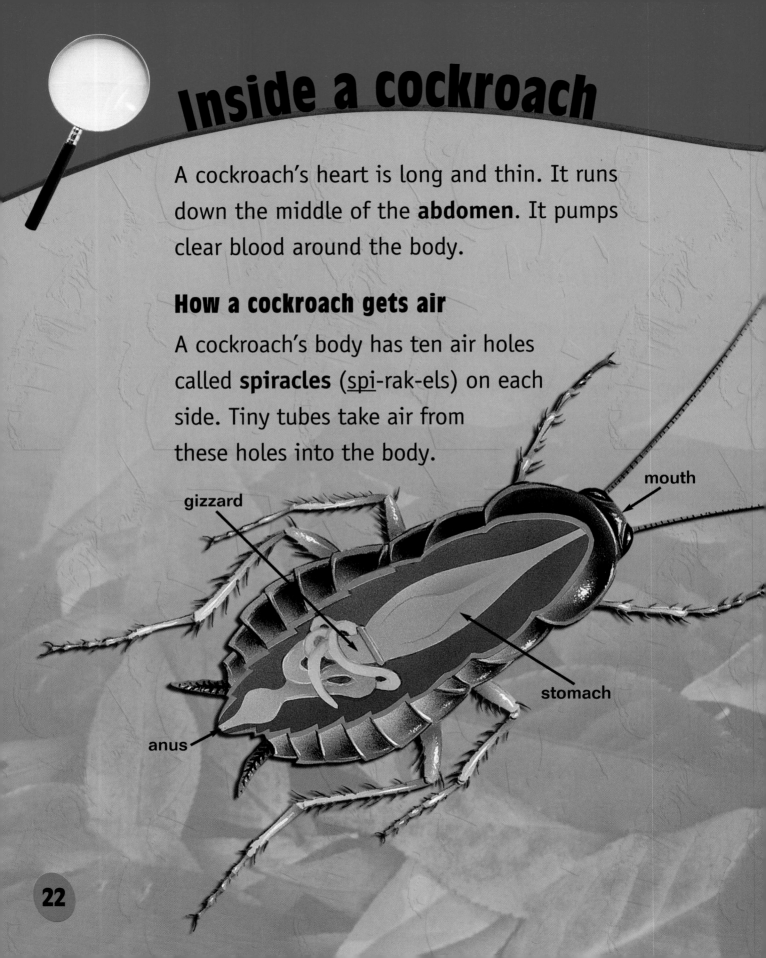

Inside a cockroach

A cockroach's heart is long and thin. It runs down the middle of the **abdomen**. It pumps clear blood around the body.

How a cockroach gets air

A cockroach's body has ten air holes called **spiracles** (<u>spi</u>-rak-els) on each side. Tiny tubes take air from these holes into the body.

gizzard

mouth

stomach

anus

What happens to food?

A cockroach's food is crushed inside the mouth. It goes down in a tube to a large stomach, which is in the first half of the abdomen. The stomach swells up when it is full of food.

Then the food enters a smaller area called a **gizzard.** The gizzard has teeth in it, which mash the food up even more. This means a cockroach can eat food with **solid** pieces in it, unlike other insects such as mosquitoes that can only feed on **liquids**.

Waste passes out of the **anus**, on the end of the abdomen.

Cockroach eggs

Cockroaches grow from eggs. A female **mates** with a male, then eggs grow inside her. In some cockroaches, the eggs hatch inside the mother. Usually, a mother cockroach lays her eggs first, and then they hatch.

Egg bag

Cockroach eggs are laid in a small egg bag. The bag has a tough skin, and it protects the eggs. It often has about 20 eggs in it.

Some female cockroaches carry the egg bags with them until the eggs hatch. Others put the bag in a safe place.

abdomen

egg bag

Hatching out

The eggs hatch inside the egg bag. The young cockroaches are called **nymphs** (nimfs). The nymphs begin to grow. The egg bag has tiny holes in it, so the nymphs can get air. When they are too big for the bag, it splits open. The cockroach nymphs come out together.

The nymphs come out of the egg bag when they grow too big for it.

Young cockroaches

When cockroach **nymphs** hatch, they are small and you can see through their skin. They have no wings, and have short **antennae** (feelers). The **exoskeleton** hardens after one or two hours, and becomes coloured.

Usually, the nymphs grow up without help from their mother.

Staying with mother

Nymphs of the Cuban burrowing cockroach stay underneath their mother, or nearby. They do not leave their mother until they have moulted twice. By this time they may be up to one month old.

A newly hatched nymph.

exoskeleton

A young cockroach with its old exoskeleton.

Growing up

As a young cockroach gets bigger, its hard exoskeleton breaks off to make room for its growing body. This is called moulting.

When a growing cockroach has just lost its old exoskeleton, it is soft and white. After a few hours, the cockroach hardens and darkens in colour. Then it eats its old exoskeleton. During moulting, a cockroach's legs, mouthparts or antennae might break off accidentally. It can grow new ones.

27

Cockroaches and us

Cockroaches sometimes come into houses, mostly in areas that are warm and wet. Cockroaches like houses because they find lots of small places in them, to rest in and to lay their eggs.

Cockroaches can be pests because they get into food, and leave their droppings behind. This is unclean, and can smell. People kill house cockroaches with poisons.

Common pests

The most common pests in houses are the American, Australian, German, Oriental and brownbanded cockroaches. All of these **species** are found in many parts of the world.

Shy cockroaches

Many people find cockroaches scary, but cockroaches do not bite or sting people. They just run away. They can look scary because they run fast and move suddenly. It is very hard to catch a cockroach, because they move away from danger very quickly.

Most cockroaches live in forests and fields. We may not often see them, but they are still there, eating whatever they can or resting in their small homes.

Some people keep cockroaches as pets.

Find out for yourself

You may be able to find a place outdoors where there are a lot of leaves, bark, branches and stones on the ground. You could gently disturb the ground-covering with a stick, and see if there are any cockroaches underneath.

Book to read
Bug Books: Cockroach, K Hartley, C Macro and Philip Taylor (Heinemann Library, 1999)

Using the Internet
Explore the Internet to find out more about cockroaches. Websites can change, so if the links below no longer work, do not worry. Use a search engine, such as www.yahooligans.com or www.internet4kids.com, and type in a keyword such as 'cockroaches', or the name of a particular cockroach.

Websites
http://yucky.kids.discovery.com/noflash/roaches/index.html
The site has all sorts of amazing facts and information about cockroaches.

http://www.ento.vt.edu/~sharov/3d/virtual.html
This site has short videos and instructions to create your own virtual cockroach.

Glossary

abdomen last of the three main sections of an insect

antenna (plural: antennae) feeler, on an insect's head

anus hole in the abdomen through which droppings are passed

compound made of smaller parts

exoskeleton hard outside skin of an insect

gizzard stomach for grinding up food

jaw hard mouthpart that moves and often has teeth on it, usually used for biting and holding food

liquid something that is runny, not hard, such as juice

mate when a male and a female come together to produce young

nocturnal active at night

nymph young stage of an insect; a nymph looks similar to the adult, except smaller

palp small body part like a finger, near an insect's mouth

predator animal that kills and eats another animal

sense how an animal knows what is going on around it

shield large, hard, flat object, usually for protection

solid hard, not runny

species type or kind of animal; animals of the same species can produce young together

spine hard, pointed spike

spiracle tiny air hole on an insect's body

temperature measure of hot and cold

thorax chest part of an insect

vein small tube in the body that carries blood; dry veins in insect wings are empty

vibration fast shaking movement

Index